THERE IS NO ONE ELSE
drama

♥

Johanna Miklós

There Is No One Else
drama

ISBN 0990636011
ISBN 978-0-9906360-1-4

Cover design by Simona Doxan

By the same author

Perfectly Pretty and other love stories

Acknowledgments

I would like to thank the writers at the virtual laboratory Zoetrope; my friend and editor Russell Bittner; Helga Schier at With Pen and Paper; and the team at The Blue Pencil led by Amy Maddox for their invaluable contributions; Simona Doxan for cover design and website design and maintenance; and my family and partner for their unconditional support.

About *There Is No One Else*

I wrote the first version of this play as my MFA thesis at The Catholic University of America. It was then called "Return to Kuta." My attempts to have it produced failed. One dramaturg returned the manuscript with the comment: "Who cares about Hungary?"

In early 1990, I reworked the play. I allowed Istvan and Arabella to meet again in the changed political landscape, and then started the whole submission process all over. The play was still called "Return to Kuta" and it still didn't interest anyone.

In 2003 I spent a few days in Budapest. A Danube River cruise was part of that experience and made its way into the play then renamed "Lies in the Soul" – and still no theatre was interested.

Loathe for Istvan and Arabella to disappear without leaving even a ripple, I decided to turn the play into a short story titled "There Is No One Else."

I even planned to include that story in my collection "Perfectly Pretty and other love stories." I thank the editors at With Pen and Paper and The Blue Pencil for their careful reading of the short story – the comments made by Helga Schier and Amy Maddox confirmed to me that this love story is best left as a play.

Synopsis

There Is No One Else is a story of love, betrayal, deceit, prejudice and tragedy. Set in Budapest, Hungary, the play tells the story of Istvan and Arabella Geza with World War II, the 1956 Uprising, and the eventual fall of Communism in 1989/90 (the Velvet Revolution) as backdrop. A three-act play with film segments interspersed between the scenes, the story begins with the penultimate scene in the winter of 1989/90 and then moves back and forth through time.

Istvan and Arabella marry in the spring of 1936. She is 17, pregnant, and from a lower class, Jewish family; he is 21 and from a wealthy, Christian family. Istvan marries Arabella over the crude and vehement protests of his father, Viktor Geza.

Together with their child, Michael, they live happily until Christmas 1944. When Istvan is drafted into the Hungarian army, he insists on sending Michael to his family's home in Kuta. Arabella remains in Budapest.

A bomb destroys Kuta, killing everyone except Michael. Neighbors return an irrevocably psychologically damaged Michael to Arabella. Almost simultaneously, the Russians take Istvan as a prisoner of war.

Istvan returns to Budapest eleven years later - October 1956. He finds Arabella, now a lawyer, living alone with Michael.

Istvan learns of his son's condition, his parents' deaths, and the destruction of Kuta. Arabella accepts him as her husband and they struggle to start again. Istvan is both devastated and embarrassed by his son's condition. He is convinced Michael would be cured if only he could be made to remember. As the Hungarian revolution explodes, Istvan prods Michael's memory with stories and photographs of the Geza family home in the village of Kuta. The shelling, however, is what jolts Michael's memory. He runs from the apartment looking for the safety of Kuta and dies on the streets of Budapest.

In the Winter of 1989/90, Arabella calls Istvan when a hospital requires her to be released to the care of a family member. When he asks why him, she tells him there is no one else left. Istvan believes in a future for them and for Hungary. Arabella is more skeptical. She cannot escape the past, especially her terrible guilt over Michael's death as she believes Michael was on the streets looking for her. In a desperate attempt to win her back, Istvan finally confesses the truth to Arabella.

Characters in Order of Appearance

TOUR GUIDE - voice over
PROSTITUTES
BUSINESSMEN
ISTVAN GEZA
ARABELLA GEZA
MAROT
MRS. MAROT
SOROS
PROHASZKA
VIKTOR GEZA
IRINA GEZA
PATAK
MARIA
VIOLINIST
BELA
JANOS
ILONA
SUSI
TIBOR
VERA
WAITER
MICHAEL GEZA
OLDER WOMAN
YOUNG MAN

2 YOUNG MEN CHANTING
3 ARMED YOUNG WOMEN
MAN
WOMAN WITH GUN
DOCTOR

FILM 1.
PRISONERS OF WAR
ISTVAN GEZA
SOVIET ARMY SOLDIERS
SOVIET ARMY OFFICER
10 YOUNG WOMEN

FILM 2.
ISTVAN GEZA
2 DOCK WORKERS

FILM 3.
PASSENGERS ON A TRAM 1956
ISTVAN GEZA
OLD WOMAN SELLING NEWSPAPERS
WAITRESS
FAT WOMAN

FILM 4.
ELEGANT COUPLES AT CAFÉ IN 1936
ARABELLA
YOUNG WOMAN
WAITER
ELDERLY COUPLE
ISTVAN GEZA
STUDENTS

FILM 5.
ISTVAN GEZA
ARABELLA GEZA

FILM 6.
ISTVAN GEZA
CLARA

FILM 7.
ISTVAN GEZA
MICHAEL GEZA

FILM 8.
MICHAEL GEZA
ISTVAN GEZA

FILM 9.
GROUPS OF PEOPLE ON THE STREETS
STUDENTS
ISTVAN GEZA
WOMAN
MICHAEL GEZA

Note: All films are SILENT and in BLACK &
WHITE

THERE IS NO ONE ELSE

Act I
Scene 1

<u>Budapest, Hungary, in the winter of 1989</u>

Slide projections on a large screen accompany the voice-over text. Projections include Buda Castle by night, Hotel Gellért, Petőfi Bridge, Liberty Bridge, Elisabeth Bridge.
Sound effects: the rumbling of a boat engine fades in and out with the voice-over of the TOUR GUIDE.

TOUR GUIDE (*voice-over*): Welcome to our Danube river cruise. We begin this historical tour of Budapest on the Buda side. On your left you see the Royal Palace, begun in the middle of the thirteenth century. A chapel and palace were added by Sigismund of Luxembourg—by the late fifteenth century, the king of Hungary's palace was one of the most splendid in Europe. At the end of World War II, it collapsed and was burnt down. The rebuilding continues. You see also the elegant Hotel Gellért—famous for thermal baths and a very impressive list of guests including politicians and film stars from all over the world. And now we pass under the

Elisabeth Bridge, also completely destroyed during World War II by the Nazis. It was reconstructed in 1964. Here, we turn around to the Pest side.

> *(Sound effect: struggling engine of a boat and water slapping against the hull.*
>
> *Set: the slides on the screens change to the opposite river bank including the promenade known as Duna Korzo that stretches from the snow-covered Sandor Petöfi statue to the parliament building. The screens disappear and reveal the base of the statue.)*

TOUR GUIDE (*voice-over continued*): At the little square on your right you see the statue of the poet Sandor Petöfi, 1823 to 1849. Petöfi is the symbol of our Hungarian revolutionary spirit. A hero of the 1848-49 revolution, he died on the battlefield fighting for Hungary's freedom.
We follow the Duna Korzo, where generations of Hungarians have gone for romantic walks with their sweethearts, and approach the parliament building. This is the symbol of Budapest. It was built in

1880. The parliament building is 300 yards long and 140 yards at its greatest width . . .

(Sound effect of boat engine fades. PROSTITUTES, wrapped in brightly colored fake fur coats, promenade—perched on shiny high heeled boots—along the Duna Korzo. SEX TOURISTS—disguised as businessmen in long winter coats—look for entertainment. There is a lively but sotto voce exchange of propositions and counter-propositions.

ISTVAN (74) and ARABELLA (71) enter. ISTVAN wears a dark winter coat, hat, gloves, and a long scarf over his best suit and shoes that pinch. ARABELLA, tired and unkempt, has only a thin, gray raincoat over a simple gray 1970s Socialist-Republics-issue frock to protect her from the cold. She carries a small, battered, cardboard suitcase. They walk past the PROSTITUTES and SEX TOURISTS to the statue. ISTVAN plops down on a step at its base, discreetly holds down the back of one shoe and lifts his heel out of it. ARABELLA hesitates and then picks a spot at a distance from ISTVAN. She clears away the snow with her bare hands and also sits.)

ISTVAN: I haven't been here in years. Hasn't changed, I don't think.
ARABELLA: Thank you.
ISTVAN: They can't keep you against your will.
ARABELLA: They tried.
ISTVAN: Well, they can't! It's your health, your life: you decide. They can only give advice—or make suggestions based on their knowledge and experience—of what they think would be best for you under the circumstances.

(He frees his second foot.)

ISTVAN: Are you okay?
ARABELLA: God, yes! *(Pause.)* Getting older, that's all.

(She observes a young PROSTITUTE flash open her coat to an OLD SEX TOURIST dressed like ISTVAN.)

ARABELLA: Old.

ISTVAN: I'm seventy-four.
ARABELLA: Yes.

(The young PROSTITUTE puts her arm around the OLD SEX TOURISTS's shoulder. He whispers a kinky wish into her ear. She laughs and waves the "naughty boy" finger at him. Exeunt.)

ISTVAN: Is there anything else I can do for you?
ARABELLA: I'll be going home. I live near here.
ISTVAN: I know.

(An older PROSTITUTE approaches ISTVAN. He shakes his head. She shrugs, targets SEX TOURISTS.)

ISTVAN: Your call surprised me - after all these years of silence.

(ARABELLA shrugs exactly like the PROSTITUTE moments before.)

ISTVAN: You didn't come to my seventieth. I sent you an invitation.

(The PROSTITUTE is joined by a second PROSTITUTE and they link arms with two SEX TOURISTS.)

ISTVAN: You missed quite a party! Great wine!
ARABELLA: I didn't come to your sixty-fifth birthday party either.
ISTVAN: No. *(Pause.)* Did you get the tulips?
ARABELLA: Pink.
ISTVAN: They delivered seventy? I ordered seventy.

(The PROSTITUTES and SEX TOURISTS exit.)

ARABELLA: Two black plastic buckets filled with pink tulips.
ISTVAN: So, you got them. *(Pause.)* These are exciting times we live in, Arabella. We're witnessing history. A time of great changes -
ARABELLA: History! Again! These "changes" as you call them are not for me. Everybody charging madly - into what? The future tense is all I hear now: we will all trade our Trabant in for a Mercedes. We had nothing to offer the world thirty years ago and we still have nothing either the Germans or Americans want. Whatever this is really

about, it's for those who still have life ahead of them.

ISTVAN: There's hope again.

(ARABELLA *points at the last exiting PROSTITUTE*.)

ARABELLA: That kind of hope? What?

ISTVAN: You were in the hospital for too long. Those white coats and grim faces depressed you.

ARABELLA: Seventy-one hard years depressed me, Istvan.

ISTVAN: Say that again.

ARABELLA: Seventy-one hard years. What?

ISTVAN: My name. You haven't called me by my name since—

ARABELLA: I haven't.

(Silence.)

(The set grows dark until there is only a cold circle of light on ISTVAN and ARABELLA.)

ISTVAN: Aren't you cold? That coat's a bit thin for this time of year.

ARABELLA: It's my good coat.

ISTVAN: It's a very nice coat, but a bit light. Would you like my scarf?

(*He struggles back into his shoes, limps over to her, takes off his long wool scarf, and wraps it carefully around her neck and shoulders.*)

ISTVAN: Better?
ARABELLA: Scratchy. And smelly.
ISTVAN: Wool. One hundred percent pure wool. (*sits*) Are you taking medication?
ARABELLA (laughs softly): Against old age? What?
ISTVAN: I mean, for the pain.
ARABELLA: I feel no pain.
ISTVAN: You were sick! You were hospitalized! You've just spent weeks swallowing pills, getting shots, were nursed. . . . What's wrong with you?
ARABELLA: Nothing special. My body's old. Parts start breaking down. Bits stop working the way they used to, you know.
ISTVAN: Anything specific?
ARABELLA: Nothing I care to talk about.
ISTVAN: Should I leave?
ARABELLA: I don't care.
ISTVAN: Why did you call me?
ARABELLA: I wanted out of that place! They wouldn't discharge me unless someone came for me. Treated me like a small child. Disgusting.
ISTVAN: Why me?

ARABELLA: There is no one else.

(Silence.)

ISTVAN: Are you lonely?
ARABELLA: No.
ISTVAN: I am. I'm so lonely, I don't even bother to think anymore.
ARABELLA: But the party! You had guests at your party! Your seventieth birthday party!
ISTVAN: I had very good wine.
ARABELLA: But, your friends—
ISTVAN: I drank the wine and waited for you. I got totally drunk. They found me on a park bench and locked me away for a while. I was an eyesore and a public disgrace. Not what is expected of a retired teacher. I was sentenced to two months out in the country. They thought I was an alcoholic. The man in the room with me was dying of syphilis.
ARABELLA: I thought you had friends.
ISTVAN: Would you have come, had you known that I was alone?
ARABELLA: Probably not.
ISTVAN: Do you know anything about my life?
ARABELLA: The last thirty-three years? Nothing. It doesn't matter.

ISTVAN: May I walk you home? Please.

ARABELLA: Home?

ISTVAN: Where you live.

ARABELLA: Very small- made just for one - a cell, really.

ISTVAN: I want to make sure you get home safely. (*Pause.*) We've been married for fifty-three years.

ARABELLA: Our marriage lasted eight years.

ISTVAN: But on paper—

ARABELLA: Paper is patient!

ISTVAN: You're the only woman I ever wanted to marry.

ARABELLA (*walks away*): And not even that is true.

> (ISTVAN *remains alone in an ever smaller circle of light.*)

ARABELLA (*impatiently out of the dark*): Are you walking me home? What?

> *Blackout*

Film 1

Heading on a white sheet of paper on a manual typewriter:

Christmas, 1944.

INT. SHACK – DAY.

Rows of superimposed bare plank beds. Emaciated and exhausted PRISONERS OF WAR in soiled and torn German, Hungarian, Austrian, and Polish WWII uniforms stand between the rows of beds. The prisoners closest to the doors of the shack look outside with blank expressions on their ravaged faces.

EXT. GATE AT CAMP 207 – URAL – DAY.

Prisoners' POV.

A RUSSIAN SOLDIER drags a heavy weight. It looks like logs.

CLOSE UP "LOGS"

Three corpses in Polish uniforms tied to a pole like slaughtered beasts.

BACK TO SCENE

The soldier drags the corpses over mud-trampled snow through the heavily guarded gate into the camp.

INT SHACK - DAY

The door to the shack is closed by two armed RUSSIAN SOLDIERS, ending the vision of the dragged corpses.

ISTVAN (here aged 30) in a tattered and soiled Hungarian Army WWII uniform grows tense. His face shows fear.

The door opens again. Russian soldiers stand by the door. The prisoners, led by Istvan, file out.

COLLAGE

Growing piles of discarded uniforms.

INT. SHACK – LATER.

The prisoners file back in. Their
heads have been roughly shorn. They
are now all wearing soiled and
padded POW "uniforms." Deprived of
hair and distinctive uniforms, they
all look alike. The prisoners look
at each other with suspicion: there
are no mirrors, but seeing the
others gives each man an idea of
what he looks like.

Two RUSSIAN SOLDIERS stand in the
door. One laughs.

CLOSE UP MOUTH

Rotten teeth.

BACK TO SCENE

TEN SOVIET FEMALE MEDICAL STUDENTS
enter the shack, flanked by armed
soldiers and the CAPTAIN of the
camp. Istvan and the other prisoners
lower their heads in shame. They are
roughly pushed into ten lines.

A soldier steps over to a plank bed
notes a muddy shoe print on the

plank. Istvan is dragged over by another soviet soldier. Behind him, the students start their "medical examination" of the POWs forced to undress before them.

EXT. CAMP 207 - DAY.

Istvan, in prisoners' clothes, pushed across the muddy snow by armed soldiers.

INT. SOLITARY CONFINEMENT SHED - DAY.

Istvan stumbles in the dark shack and the door closes behind him.

Act I

Scene 2

Budapest, 1944

Set: entrance, large dining room and salon of the GEZAS' elegant apartment. The heavy curtains are drawn. A lamp with a lamp shade matching the curtains casts light on Biedermeier chairs, a deep nineteenth-century sofa, and a low Oriental coffee table. The dining room part has a large, heavily carved dark wood table and four high backed chairs. On a very ornate cabinet against the wall are a silver tea set and a silver-framed photograph of ISTVAN and ARABELLA with a baby. There is a bookcase filled with leather bound books and there are paintings on the walls by late nineteenth- and early twentieth-century Hungarian artists. The entrance door has a modern art, stained-glass upper half; beside it are a discreet coat rack and an ornate umbrella stand. From the entrance there is a corridor to what is assumed to be the kitchen and bathroom and another door to MICHAEL's bedroom. From the salon there are double doors to the master bedroom.

The lights come up very slowly with the sound effect of the low rumble of a boat engine, water slapping against its hull.

TOUR GUIDE (*voice-over*): In March 1944 Nazi troops occupied and plundered Hungary. They destroyed all bridges and turned Budapest into a battlefield. The Soviet Army's siege of Budapest then began Christmas 1944 with air raids . . .

(The low rumble of the boat turns into that of approaching heavy WWII bombers. Sirens wail. Explosion—a bomb hits a nearby building. Lights flicker.

Sudden BLACKOUT and SILENCE.

Sudden wail of Sirens.

Sudden SILENCE.

Soft knocking on the stained-glass panes of the entrance door. The lights on the set come back on.

ARABELLA (here aged 27) enters from the master bedroom in stocking feet and a simple but good-quality 1940s dress. The knocking becomes louder.

ARABELLA stands in the salon, uncertain of what to do. The knocking turns to pounding. ARABELLA runs to the entrance.)

ARABELLA (*loud whisper*): What is it?
MAROT (*offstage*): Mrs. Arabella Geza?
ARABELLA: What do you want?
MRS. MAROT (*offstage*): Are you Mrs. Geza?

(ARABELLA opens the door. MAROT—an older man in clean peasant clothes—and his wife, MRS. MAROT—not so clean—step into the apartment half dragging, half carrying MICHAEL GEZA (aged 9) between them. The boy is wrapped in a dirty blanket. ARABELLA screams.)

MRS. MAROT: It's her son. I told you so. It's the son of the son of Viktor Geza.
ARABELLA: Michael! My little life!

(She covers the boy's face with kisses. MICHAEL does not react.)

MAROT (*bowing*): Marot. I'm Janos Marot from Kuta. That's my wife.

ARABELLA: Why aren't you saying anything, Michael? Aren't you happy to see me? It's all over now! You're with me. Do you want to cry? Go ahead—even a big boy like you is allowed to cry. Are you cold?

(*She holds him tightly in her arms and rocks him back and forth.*)

ARABELLA: What is wrong with my child?

MAROT: We think it's the shock—

MRS. MAROT: A bomb flattened the main house. Why they bombed our village—who the hell knows? There's nothing left of the Geza home.

ARABELLA: Look at me, Michael.

MAROT: He's the only survivor.

ARABELLA: My mother-in-law? Viktor Geza?

MRS. MAROT: Your boy's alive because they protected him. Everybody else in that basement died

MAROT: We found him under their bodies, under the rubble.

ARABELLA: They loved you.

MAROT: We'd have kept him until the war is over . . . the Gezas were always very good to us and every war does end. . . Mrs. Geza especially, you know. Always a kind word.

MRS. MAROT: We've got seven of our own to feed! How do you want to look after that? Like I haven't enough to do!

MAROT: Shut up!

MRS. MAROT: We had a terrible time getting here. If it weren't for how generous the Gezas have always been . . . There won't be any bridges left in Budapest. That's what they're aiming at. We've got to get back, Janos—somehow!

ARABELLA: I understand. I'm grateful to you for going through all this trouble. Please, I'd like to thank you, to give you something.

> (*She leaves MICHAEL on the sofa, takes a small painting from the wall, and holds it out to MRS.MAROT, who stares past ARABELLA at the silver.*)

MAROT: It's not necessary, Mrs. Geza. These are hard—

> (*MRS. MAROT grabs the silver teapot*)

MRS.MAROT: It's getting late.

(She runs out the door with the silver .)

ARABELLA *(softly)*: That was my mother's.
MAROT: God with you, Mrs. Geza.
ARABELLA: With us all, Marot.

(MAROT closes the door.)

ARABELLA : Are you in pain, my baby? How you have grown! How thin you are!

(Arabella lifts his legs, makes him lie down. She turns off the lamp, sits down, and gently lifts MICHAEL'S head onto her lap.)

ARABELLA: I love you with all my heart, my little boy.

(Sound effect of a WWII bomber approaching and flying over. MICHAEL screams as the plane flies over.)

Blackout

Film 2

Heading on a white sheet of paper on a manual typewriter:

Coming home in October, 1956

EXT. STEAMBOAT ON THE DANUBE – DAY

Istvan (here aged 41) wearing a large hat and an oversized coat, stands at the railing looking down into the water.

EXT. DOCK IN BUDAPEST – DAY.

The steamboat docks. TWO DOCK WORKERS attach the ropes of the boat on the dock. Behind the men, a mangy cat eats the remains of a sparrow.

Istvan steps off the boat. He stops beside the cat and takes a piece of paper from his pocket, reads it and then keeps walking, the paper tucked back into his pocket.

EXT. WROUGHT IRON GATES - PEST 1956

COLLAGE:

Istvan walks past many gates and houses badly damaged by the war. Some are undergoing repair work. He stops at a large gate.

INT. SCHOOL AUDITORIUM - DAY

Istvan stands in front of two large commemorative plaques. One, tarnished with age, has the dates 1914 - 1918 at the top followed by a long list of names in alphabetical order. The second plaque shines with newness and has the dates 1939 - 1945 at the top. Istvan looks with sadness at the names he reads there. He touches the name "Geza, Istvan."

Act 1
Scene 3

<u>Budapest, 1956</u>

The lights come up slowly during the voice-over and sound effects of the low rumbling of a boat engine and water slapping against the hull.

The set: an office with functional gray furniture on a square, gray platform lit by 1950s industrial lamps.

Suspended above the set there is an absurdly large page from a daily calendar: 14 in huge print and in smaller print underneath: October

TOUR GUIDE (*voice over*): Look up to the citadel on your left. There, you see the Liberation Monument erected in 1947 in honor of the Soviet army. The figure holds high the palm of victory . . .

> *(Fade out of the voice-over and the sound effects.*

SOROS, a government employee in an ill-fitting gray suit, is napping at his desk.

ISTVAN GEZA, dressed as in Film #2, sits down opposite SOROS. He takes off his hat and fidgets with it on his lap. He waits.)

SOROS (*snaps to attention*): What can I do for you?
ISTVAN (*jumps to his feet*): Geza, Istvan. I was told to come to you. Room 4b. I'm alive, you see.
SOROS: Got you. (*He reaches under the desk and heaves up an absurdly large gray folder.*) What did you say was your name?
ISTVAN: Geza, Istvan. G-E-Z-A-I-S-T-V-A-N.

(SOROS takes a huge gray pencil, sharpens it with a tiny pocket knife, and starts to fill out a form in the folder.)

SOROS: We are the . . . fourteenth. Born?
ISTVAN: Yes.
SOROS: When were you born and where were you born? It's for the formalities. I personally couldn't care less.
ISTVAN: I'm sorry. I haven't tried humor in a long time. Budapest. November 7, 1915.

SOROS: Seven and fifteen. Right. Since when? When were you declared dead? By whom?

ISTVAN: I don't know.

SOROS: Then why do you come and bother me? How do you know you're dead when you don't know—

ISTVAN: My name's on the list. I'm on the commemorative plaque in my alma mater— my old school. In memoriam. But here I am! I have to clear that up, don't I? I mean, they wouldn't have put my name on there unless they were pretty sure that I'm dead—or at least declared not alive. I want to fix—

SOROS: You really don't know when—

ISTVAN: I just got back.

SOROS: Relatives. Usually relatives take care of such things.

ISTVAN: I haven't had time. I haven't had time to look for them. I just got back.

SOROS: From the Soviet Union?

ISTVAN: Russia. Yes.

(*He takes his release papers from his pockets and hands them to SOROS*)

SOROS (*reading*): Useful. Very useful. I will naturally have to have this translated.

ISTVAN: They concern my release.

(SOROS jumps to his feet, quickly checks the four corners of the platform, returns to his desk, and takes a photograph out of a drawer.)

SOROS: My brother, Imre. Maybe you saw him there? Soros. Soros, Imre.
ISTVAN: Too many years.
SOROS : We haven't heard from him since fifty-one. That was the last Red Cross letter from him.
ISTVAN: There were just too many faces.

(Sound effect of approaching footsteps. SOROS hides the photograph and opens the folder again. Sound effect of retreating footsteps.)

SOROS: Where will you be staying?
ISTVAN: I . . . I don't know.
SOROS: You have to live somewhere.
ISTVAN: I don't have any money.
SOROS: Family.
ISTVAN: I have to find my family.
SOROS: Here?
ISTVAN: I don't know. Maybe. Maybe they're in Budapest.
SOROS: When were you taken prisoner?
ISTVAN: At the end.

SOROS: Forty-four? Forty-five? Later?

ISTVAN: In uniform, Christmas 1944. It was cold and we knew the war was lost and I was hungry. So hungry!

ISTVAN: I thought I was hungry. I learned about real hunger later. The Russians taught me that. I wanted to eat and there was this farm ahead of me . . . I wanted to shoot a chicken . . . It was the only shot I fired during the war! A chicken! Can you imagine?

SOROS: And?

ISTVAN: I missed. I've been hungry for a long time.

SOROS: Some things haven't changed in the last eleven years.

ISTVAN: Can you help me?

SOROS: I need to fill out this form. Where will you be . . . ?

ISTVAN: Please. I don't know where they are—if they are . . .

(Soros heaves an enormous telephone book on his desk.)

SOROS: Name?

ISTVAN: The same. Geza.

SOROS (*flipping pages*): Geza. You said: Geza . . . here is Geza. . Geza A.

ISTVAN: My wife. Arabella.

SOROS (*writing*): Nagymezö Eleven.

ISTVAN: What are you doing! What are you writing?

SOROS: The address: Nagymezö Eleven. It's here in Pest, just off–

ISTVAN: I know where Nagymezö Street is! But I don't know whether I can live there!

SOROS: You have to live somewhere.

ISTVAN: I was gone for eleven years. Eleven years! Don't you understand?

SOROS: We have to be able to contact you. There will be questions. You need someone to identify you . . . have to be sure you are who you say you are. . .

ISTVAN: She was the only Arabella? In Budapest. What about other cities? Do you have that information?

SOROS: Well, we're fairly well organized.

ISTVAN: Could you check just one more? Please.

SOROS: Where?

ISTVAN: Kuta. It's a village. My family is from there, you see. The house and the land and the people . . . I haven't been there since thirty-six . . . in Kuta.

Blackout

Film 3

Heading on a white sheet of paper on a manual typewriter:
October, 1956

Slowly typed in the center of the paper:
Arabella

INT. CROWDED TRAM - DAY.

Istvan, wearing hat and coat, is on the tram looking out a window.

Istvan's POV.
Gray streets of Pest. MEN and WOMEN hurry along.

INT. CROWDED TRAM - CONT.
Istvan looks around at the other PASSENGERS. In the back of the tram he spots a young couple. The YOUNG MAN kisses the YOUNG WOMAN. The woman sees Istvan observing them and pushes the young man playfully away.

EXT. TRAM STOP/STREET - SAME.

Istvan gets off the tram among other PASSENGERS. He buys the newspaper "Igazság" from an OLD WOMAN.

INT. COFFEEHOUSE – DAY.

Istvan stands hesitantly in the door.

A WAITRESS in black dress with a white apron motions him to a small table. Istvan sits down and clumsily opens the paper. The waitress sets down a coffee and a glass of water.

Insert:

Chipped cup and soup spoon on chipped saucer. Water glass with traces of lipstick.

Back to scene:

Istvan flips the pages of the newspaper. Frustrated, he folds it sloppily and drops it on the floor. Istvan drinks the coffee,

CONT.

CONTINUED

rummages in his coat pockets, puts a forint (Hungarian currency) on the table.

EXT. STREETS OF PEST - 1956 - DAY

COLLAGE:

Istvan walks past buildings in the back streets of Pest.

INT. HOUSE ENTRANCE - DAY.

Istvan stands in front of mailboxes reading the names. A small FAT WOMAN with a fat dog squeezes past him.

Insert:

Mailbox with 'Geza, A.' It is very noticeable that a printed 'I' was turned into an 'A' by hand.

INT. STAIRWAY.

Istvan slowly makes his way up dirty marble steps. The wrought iron banister is broken in parts, and paint peels off the walls. Istvan runs out of breath and leans against the wall. He is perspiring and wipes the sweat from his brow with his sleeves.

INT. LANDING AND ENTRANCE TO GEZA APARTMENT

Istvan stands in front of the door with art nouveau stained glass panels. His face is wet with perspiration. His eyes are feverish. His lips are pressed together in a thin line. ISTVAN makes a fist with his right hand and raises the fist.

Act I

Scene 4

Budapest, October 14, 1956

Set: Apartment of Arabella Geza. Evening.

Heavy silk curtains frame a view onto treetops and part of the facade of the Fővárosi Operettszínház [Operetta Theatre]. The lamp with silk lamp shade matching the curtains casts light on uncomfortable Biedermeier chairs, the deep nineteenth-century sofa, and the low Oriental coffee table on which there is a pile of newspapers and journals.

In the dining room area, the carved dark wood table is covered with a lace tablecloth and the four high-backed chairs have colorful embroidered shawls draped over them. On the very ornate cabinet against the wall, the silver framed photographs of ISTVAN and ARABELLA with a baby and with friends have been joined by a few simply framed photographs of ARABELLA with a teenage MICHAEL and an elderly gentleman. Herend china and crystal glasses are in place and a simple china pot has joined the remaining silver tea set.

The bookcases are still filled with leather bound books and many paperback books have been added. The paintings on the walls by late nineteenth- and early twentieth-century Hungarian artists have not changed. On the discreet coat rack is PROHASZKA's heavy man's coat, a smart businesslike coat, and a silk head scarf belonging to ARABELLA. There is a solitary black umbrella in the stand.

Minimal light on the set.

Sound effect: low rumble of a boat engine.

The Housekeeper PROHASZKA cleans with a feather duster.

TOUR GUIDE (*voice-over fades in*): Hungarian history is filled with conquerors and oppressors: Turks, Austrians, Germans, Russians . . . and Hungarians fighting the oppressors. Before the Velvet Revolution of 1989, there was the uprising of October-November 1956. It was an attempt by the Hungarian people to obtain more autonomy from Soviet rule and it failed. Before that, the war of 1848-49 against Habsburg absolutism . . . (*Voice-over fades out.*)

(Sound effects end.

There is a knock on the glass panel of the entrance door. PROHASZKA waddles over and opens the door a crack.)

PROHASZKA: Yes?
ISTVAN: I'd like to talk to Arabella Geza. She does live here?
PROHASZKA: Who are you and what do you want?
ISTVAN: Tell Mrs. Geza a gentleman wishes to talk to her.
PROHASZKA: Gentlemen have names!

(She slams the door shut.
ISTVAN keeps knocking.
PROHASZKA ignores it. ISTVAN continues insistently knocking on the glass panes of the door.)

PROHASZKA *(ripping the door open)*: What?!
ISTVAN: Please tell Mrs. Geza her husband is here.
PROHASZKA: How dare you! Mr. Geza is dead. Mrs. Geza is a lady with no time for crude jokes.

(ARABELLA -here aged 38- enters.)

ISTVAN: This is not a joke. Please, I have to talk—
PROHASZKA: Go away!

(She *tries to shut the door.*)

ARABELLA: What's going on, Prohaszka?
PROHASZKA: I tried to stop him . . . barging in like that! I'll get the police.   Plenty of armed guys on the streets these days.
ARABELLA (*softly*): Istvan?

(ARABELLA instinctively raises her arms to embrace ISTVAN and then drops them.)

PROHASZKA: Your husband?

(PROHASZKA exits.)

ARABELLA: Istvan.
ISTVAN : How are you? May I . . . may I sit down? I need your help, Arabella. I need a place to stay and someone to identify me.
ARABELLA: Istvan. It's really you. I'm not dreaming. No. In my dreams your return was different. Istvan. Come in. Make yourself at . . .stupid. What is the right thing to say? I have so many questions.

(Silence.)

ISTVAN: Russia. *(Pause.)* Yesterday. *(Pause.)* To see you again.
(ISTVAN takes off his coat. He is painfully thin. ARABELLA gasps.)

ISTVAN *(drily)*: Stalin's hospitality.
ARABELLA : Your last letter arrived eleven years ago.
ISTVAN : I was a prisoner of war. An animal.

(He starts to cry. ARABELLA hugs him gently. They sit next to each other on the sofa crying.)

ARABELLA *(whispers)*: I have so much to tell you. You were my best friend! I missed you!
ISTVAN: Is our son alive? And my parents?
ARABELLA: Kuta was destroyed. A stray bomb. Why would anybody bomb a farm house? Your parents were buried under the rubble.
ISTVAN: And Michael?
ARABELLA: Could you . . . could you get me a glass of water? Through here and on your—
ISTVAN: I remember.

(ISTVAN exits. ARABELLA struggles to regain her composure until ISTVAN re- enters.)

ISTVAN: Prohaszka recommends Pálinka.

(They sit down again. ISTVAN on the sofa, ARABELLA on a chair. He pours. ARABELLA throws back her drink.)

ISTVAN: So, tell me.

ARABELLA: Eleven years. That's a very long time.

ISTVAN: March '44—that's when—

ARABELLA: Your mother took my child away to Kuta.

ISTVAN: I thought Michael would be safer out in the country.

ARABELLA: Without his Jewish mother.

ISTVAN: We wanted to protect our son. My mother also understood that. Did my father—

ARABELLA: I think he loved Michael. A small Istvan for him. A second chance.

ISTVAN: Where was Michael when Kuta was destroyed and my parents were killed?

(Silence.)

ISTVAN: My parents were killed. Where was my son?

(Silence.)

ARABELLA: You didn't care for eleven years and now you demand all the answers! By what right? If I had kept a journal, I could put eleven volumes into your lap! All my pains, all my dreams, all the boring details of surviving one day after the other. You could read them, day by day. You would know it all then, every intimate detail. How I longed for you. (*Pause.*) How I hated you. You went to war and gave our only child to your mother. I was so alone and I hated you.

(Silence.)

ISTVAN: I'm sorry.

(ARABELLA slips to her knees before him and puts her head on his lap.)

ARABELLA: Remember, you held my hair in your fist when you slept? I could never get up without waking you. (*Pause.*)

ARABELLA: On my thirtieth birthday I put on the pink dress you liked so much and went to a party friends gave for me.
(*Pause.*)

There was a man there who liked me and I took him home into our bed.

(*ISTVAN pushes her away.*)

ISTVAN: Michael. Tell me about my son.
ARABELLA: He's beautiful.
ISTVAN: Tell me about his life.
ARABELLA: You don't really care. When did that stop? The caring, I mean. Was it before you left? When you gave our son away? Was it at the front? Or was it when you were captured? When did I become not worth writing to?
ISTVAN: Where is he?
ARABELLA: Working. (*Pause.*) He's part of a team. (*Pause.*) For the railways.
ISTVAN: As an engineer?

(*ARABELLA starts to giggle and then collapses into a chair laughing hysterically. Her laughter is infectious and ISTVAN joins in. She stops abruptly.*)

ARABELLA: I hate you. Michael was buried under the walls of your precious Kuta. He was found under the bodies of your dead parents. Michael was given the gift of everlasting childhood.

ISTVAN: I don't understand.

ARABELLA: Who does? (*Pause.*) Doctors say it's the shock. His mind refuses to mature, or something like that. We've tried everything. We just don't know enough about the mind, the soul, whatever . . .

ISTVAN (*sinking into himself, devastated*): He's an idiot. That's what you're trying to tell me.

ARABELLA: That is how you would put it. Michael is my son. The child you're looking for doesn't exist anymore.

ISTVAN: Does he remember me?

ARABELLA: No. He's forgotten everything. He's one of the few—the lucky few—who don't remember the war.

> (*ISTVAN picks up her glasses from the coffee table. PROHASZKA waddles from the kitchen to the entrance and grabs her coat.*)

ISTVAN: You didn't need glasses then.

ARABELLA: I also color my hair and wear a corset now.

41

PROHASZKA: I'm off. Any extras for tomorrow?
ARABELLA: Thank you, Prohaszka. Breakfast, if there's anything in the shops.
PROHASZKA (*opening the door*): Plus one, I guess.

(PROHASZKA exits)

ISTVAN: What did she mutter?
ARABELLA: She thinks you'll be here tomorrow.
ISTVAN: So did the man at City Hall.
ARABELLA: What man?
ISTVAN: Soros. Where I had to declare my existence.
ARABELLA: I only did that last year. I waited ten years.
ISTVAN (*attempting humor*): Very literary of you.
ARABELLA: I didn't start weaving.
ISTVAN: But there were suitors.
ARABELLA: You still haven't turned gray. But there are deep lines around your eyes and your mouth. And you're so very thin. Your eyes . . . weren't they darker?

ISTVAN: I've also lost a few teeth, and those that are left are all loose. Every morning we had to stand in line and get our ass pinched; whoever still had some fat on his buttocks was declared fit to work.
ARABELLA: You can sleep here. I'll fix the sofa for you.

(She exits.)

ISTVAN *(calls)*: When does Michael get in?
ARABELLA *(offstage)*: Late. It depends on where they're working. Do you have—
ISTVAN: Nothing.
ARABELLA *(stands in the doorway)*: I gave your things away.
ISTVAN: Last year? They wouldn't fit me anymore.

(ARABELLA exits.
ISTVAN takes off his shoes and slowly wanders around the room.
ARABELLA returns with a pillow and sheets.)

ARABELLA: You look tired.
ISTVAN *(laughs)*: I just wanted to say the same thing to you.
ARABELLA: I'm exhausted. The bathroom—

ISTVAN: Next to the kitchen. (*Pause.*) I'll get work. As soon as I have my papers, I'll find work. I don't want to be a burden.

ARABELLA : We'll talk about it tomorrow.

ISTVAN (*touching her arm*): Thank you. Thank you for not throwing me out.

> (*He leaves his hand on her arm. The touch turns into a timid caress.*)

ARABELLA: Throw you out? I could never throw you out.

> (*Very slowly ISTVAN takes ARABELLA into his arms. They kiss.*
>
> *The lights slowly fade.*
>
> *Sound effects: rumble of boat engine, water lapping, engine reverses.*)

TOUR GUIDE (*voice-over*): We hope you enjoyed your boat trip through Budapest and its history and wish you a pleasant stay in our capital. As we say in Hungarian: viszontlátásra—we look forward to seeing you again.

Blackout

Act II

Scene 1

<u>Budapest, Hungary, Winter of 1989</u>

A much reduced version of the 1956 apartment. There is a window with a view of a dirty wall. Very little gray light comes in through this window that has 1960s-design cheap curtains. Behind a drab curtain is the kitchenette. A narrow door leads to what must be the bathroom and a wider door is the entrance.

> *ISTVAN - dressed only his coat, sits on the bed, smoking. ARABELLA brings two mugs from the curtained-off kitchenette.*

ARABELLA: When did you start that?
ISTVAN: Do you mind?
ARABELLA: I don't have an ashtray.

> *(ISTVAN opens the small window behind the bed, throws out the cigarette, and closes it again. ARABELLA hands him a mug.)*

ARABELLA: Tea.
ISTVAN: Thank you.
ARABELLA: I haven't bought coffee in years.
ISTVAN: It's expensive.

ARABELLA: Not good for you either.
*(ARABELLA exits and returns with
a newspaper. She hands him half.)*

ARABELLA: And then we'll switch.

*(They read in silence. Then ISTVAN
mutters.)*

ARABELLA: What? Did you say something?
ISTVAN (*reads*):Borozgatank apammal;
        Ivott a jo öreg,
        s a kedvemért ez egyszer—
        az Isten aldja meg!
ARABELL (*recites*):
        Soka nem voltam otthon,
        oly rég nem lata mar,
        ugy megvénült azota—
        hja, az idö lejar.
Why are you crying? Because I can still
quote Petöfi Sandor? We learned his poems
in school, remember?
ISTVAN: "Hja, az idö lejar"—time really does
pass. Do you remember when we first
shared a newspaper?

(Arabella hides behind her paper.)

ISTVAN: Bella. What do you call home?
Hm? Do you call this room a home? I live in

a hole. A very decent place, by Hungarian standards. (*Pause.*) You kept our old things.

ARABELLA: As best I could. And what would I have exchanged them for? Cheap modern furniture that's uncomfortable to boot? (*Pause.*) You're thinking of Kuta.

ISTVAN: That was a home.

ARABELLA: Yours. I was never welcome there.

ISTVAN: I want it back. I want my family home back.

ARABELLA: What? What do you want back?

ISTVAN: Everything! The fields, the trees, the house: I want my home!

ARABELLA: Poor man.

ISTVAN: I mean it, Bella. It belonged to my family for generations and by law, I am the rightful—

ARABELLA: What right? The house was destroyed forty-five years ago. The fields have since been labored by others — not even the trees are the same. What on earth would you do there?

ISTVAN: It's my home. I belong there.

ARABELLA: Maybe that's true. Maybe you do belong there. But so do others now. Think of those who live and work there for the last forty years. That's two generations. That's lots of people who know nothing of the past you want back. Two generations raised on communist ideals and you want to show up as the rightful heir to what they believe to be their home?

ISTVAN: I could buy it back.

ARABELLA: All of it?!

ISTVAN: No. I could buy back a corner - just a small plot of my inheritance. Come with me.

ARABELLA: Where to?

ISTVAN: To Kuta.

ARABELLA: No! (*Pause.*) But if that is your dream, go. Go and pitch a tent on your father's land.

ISTVAN: I won't go alone.

ARABELLA: I wasn't welcome there when we were young.

ISTVAN: That's the past. I ask you now, come with me.

Blackout

Film 4

On a white sheet of paper on a manual typewriter:

Romance — Spring 1936

EXT. TERRACE HOTEL GELLERT - DAY.

It is a glorious spring day. ELEGANT COUPLES occupy the tables. There are vases with tulips on all the tables.

ARABELLA (here aged 17, with very long hair) sits with a pretty FRIEND who has fashionably short hair. They are both wearing small hats and white gloves. They take off their gloves as a WAITER brings ice cream. They SMILE at the sheer pleasure of being.

Next table.

An ELDERLY COUPLE leaves and a small group of STUDENTS (all male) rushes to take the table. One of the students is ISTVAN (here aged 21). He carries a newspaper under his arm.

Arabella's table

Arabella listens with a pained smile to her friend's constant babbling. She steals glances at Istvan.

<u>Istvan's table</u>

Istvan reads his newspaper. The other young men are having an animated conversation.

<u>CU – Istvan</u>

He looks up and grins.

<u>CU- Arabella</u>

Arabella lowers her eyes—he caught her watching him.

<u>Arabella's table</u>

Istvan comes to the table, bows politely and gives half his newspaper to Arabella.

Act II
Scene 2

Geza property in Kuta, September, 1936

It is a bright and cheerful autumn in the country.

Set: the walled-in yard and part of the house, with a large gate through which a "gemeskut" [Hungarian well] can be seen. Tables and benches are set for a festivity under trees heavy with chestnuts.

> *VIKTOR GEZA (50) is seated on a bench by the house.*

VIKTOR (*yells*): Irina! Where's my shirt?
IRINA (*off stage*): Which one?
VIKTOR (*shouts*): The new one.
IRINA (*off*): I put it on your bed.
VIKTOR (*yells*): Irina!
IRINA (*off*): Yes!
VIKTOR: What's there to eat?

> *(IRINA (45) a beautiful woman in sensible clothes, comes from the house carrying two jugs of wine.)*

IRINA: You're still hungry?
VIKTOR: What are you carrying?

IRINA: Wine. Are you really hungry? We just ate!

VIKTOR: And thirsty! Of course, I'm hungry! I'm a full grown man—takes more than a bowl of soup to fill me up.

IRINA: I just took a cake from the oven—but that's still hot.

VIKTOR : What are you doing in the kitchen? We have a cook and maids!

IRINA: I like to bake. How about kolbasz and bread?

VIKTOR: Do I look like a shepherd to you? All the decent food is being held back for the greedy lot to come and stuff themselves later.

IRINA: You invited them!

(Sound effects: horses' hooves and neighing.)

PATAK (*offstage*): What a bad tempered woman you are.

VIKTOR: She's giving them a hard time! I don't think I'll sell her.

(He goes to the gate to observe the stable hands with the horses behind the wall)

VIKTOR: That's my beauty! Hey, Patak! Try being gentle with her. It sometimes works with horses too. Hey, Istvan!

(Sound effects: neighing and hooves clattering.)

IRINA: He's not here yet. Would you like some wine?
VIKTOR: Well, where is he? Running around with that Jewish whore again, huh?

(IRINA silently pours wine.)

VIKTOR: Istvan! Well, where is he?
IRINA: I don't know. I'm sure he'll arrive soon.
VIKTOR: I can guess where he is! Getting that conniving slut pregnant, that's what he's up to!

(IRINA escapes to the house.)

VIKTOR: Stop being so sensitive! Married to me for twenty-five years and still a prude! Nothing but liquids for the old man! I still have all my teeth, Irina!

(MARIA (20) a maid, enters with baskets of bread.)

VIKTOR: I want something to chew!

(Sound effects: A violin, off stage, playing a traditional Hungarian tune. MARIA avoids his lunge at her/ the bread. Giggling, she quickly sets down the baskets on the tables and runs back into the house as the VIOLINIST in traditional attire comes through the gate. He is followed by the guests. Among them:

BELA and JANOS — young men; ILONA and SUSI — young women; TIBOR — an older man; VERA — an older woman; PATAK — the stable hand. The VIOLINIST bows in greeting. The guests hum the melody as they file in and shake hands with VIKTOR. IRINA comes from the house. IRINA and VIKTOR sit on a bench and listen to the music. The song ends and all applaud.)

BELA: That was something for the old! Play for us now!
ILONA: So we can dance!
IRINA: A czardas—that's for evcrybody.

(MARIA comes from the house with a huge tray on which there are bowls of pickled cucumbers, tomatoes, and peppers. The VIOLINIST starts to play a csardas. MARIA sets down the bowls. BELA pulls SUSI to dance in the space between the tables. ILONA dances with JANOS. PATAK grabs MARIA around the waist and spins her into the dance. All but TIBOR, VERA, VIKTOR GEZA, and IRINA dance. The VIOLINIST leads the cheerfully dancing pairs out through the gate.)

TIBOR (*approaching VIKTOR*): I saw a lively filly on the way . . .

VIKTOR: She's not for sale.

VERA: Just as well! I don't like nasty horses.

VIKTOR: She's fiery, not nasty! But it takes a man to see the difference. Have some wine, Vera. (*to Irina*) Food ready?

IRINA: Almost.

(VIKTOR pours wine for his guests.

Sound effects: the music played behind the wall and the young people dancing and shouting.)

TIBOR (*raising his mug*): To life!

VIKTOR: To Kuta! And to beautiful women!

(TIBOR, VERA, and VIKTOR drink. VIKTOR hands his mug to IRINA who smiles at him and takes a sip. Attracted by the music, VERA and TIBOR go to the gate to watch.)

VIKTOR : See, Irina, everybody's happy. There's life here today! Wine, a little music . . . let's join them. Let's dance!
IRINA : I haven't danced in years! (*She resists his pull.*) No, no. Viktor! I can't!
VIKTOR: Then I'll go alone, show these young chaps a step or two. What do you say, Tibor?

(The VIOLINIST appears at the gate. TIBOR and VERA dance and are joined by the young couples. VIKTOR taps PATAK on the shoulder and continues dancing with MARIA out through the gate. PATAK shrugs but keeps an eye on them. The VIOLINIST and other

dancing couples follow VIKTOR and MARIA out through the gate again. The music slowly fades.

ISTVAN -aged 21- enters.)

IRINA: Your father already missed you. He's out there dancing! Go and greet him.
ISTVAN: I'd like to talk to you first.
IRINA: Then sit and have something to drink. I have to check what's going on in the kitchen. I'll be right back.

(IRINA exits.

VIKTOR, enters.).

VIKTOR: I need a rest! Well, here he is. My son. Pour me one! Where's your mother?
ISTVAN: She wanted to check on the kitchen.
VIKTOR : What's she constantly hiding in the kitchen for? She's to be with the guests! Irina!

(TIBOR enters.)

TIBOR: Viktor! We need you for this dance. My wife says you're lighter on her feet than I am.

(VERA enters.)

VERA: Hello, Istvan. I married a clod! Your father's a better dancer than all the young chaps hopping around out there.
VIKTOR: Be right there. You're coming.
ISTVAN: I'll wait for mother.
VIKTOR: As you wish. (*To Tibor and Vera*) Coming! I won't disappoint a lovely lady.

(Exeunt.

Sound effects: The violin starts a new tune. There is stomping and clapping offstage. The music slowly fades.

IRINA comes from the house with a chunk of cake on a plate.
IRINA: Your father's enjoying himself.
ISTVAN: Drinking, dancing, yelling.
IRINA: Cake for you to taste. Careful, it's still hot.
ISTVAN: I wish—ouch! I wish he were more like you.
IRINA : He has his good sides.
ISTVAN: Where? Mm! The cake is good! Have you tried it?
IRINA : What did you want to talk about?
ISTVAN: Arabella's going to have a baby.
IRINA: Yours?

ISTVAN: I expected that question from father, not from you! Arabella loves me. Only me! Naturally, I am the father!

Irina: I'm sorry. (*Pause.*) What are you going to do?

ISTVAN: I married her. We were married yesterday.

IRINA: She's only seventeen!

ISTVAN: Her parents gave their consent.

IRINA: I would have liked to be there. You're my son. Didn't you want me there?

> (*ISTVAN puts his arms around his mother.*)

ISTVAN: I wanted you to know. Yes, I would have liked to have you there. But then father would have known and I was afraid he would have stopped it.

IRINA: You were alone. Taking such a huge step on your own! Don't you think, we should have talked about it? Maybe even with your father. He loves you! What must her parents think of us? They were not surprised that . . .

> (*Sound effects: music and laughter approaching the gate.*)

IRINA: And now? How are you going to survive? You're still a student, completely dependent on your father! I wish I had my own income.

ISTVAN: I have to tell him. Maybe, now that it's done, he'll accept my decision . . . What else can I do? I have no choice! Sooner or later, he would find out and it's better he hears it from me than from a stranger! And we have to live on something: my studies aren't finished and . . . it's going to ruin the day, isn't it? And you worked so hard. I'm sorry.

IRINA: Never mind that. Anyway, I had help in the kitchen. What matters is your life and your happiness. Where is she now?

ISTVAN: Waiting in the car with Uncle Balasz.

IRINA: My brother would be in on this! Oh, Istvan! (*Pause.*) Your father really loves you. There isn't a day when he doesn't speak of you.

ISTVAN: Have you heard him talk about Jews?

IRINA: Maybe for your sake . . . he won't want to lose his only son! He's so proud of you!

ISTVAN: I hope that you're right. Maybe he loves me enough to accept Arabella and our baby.

IRINA: Try to understand him as well. He comes from an era when the father was a god in his family.

ISTVAN: And we've discovered that he's just human?

IRINA: Sometimes even a little ridiculous and sad.

(VIKTOR enters.)

VIKTOR: I knew it! I'm dancing my heart out with the wenches and my family is secretly polishing off the cake!

IRINA: There's enough for everyone.

VIKTOR: Stop jumping around! Time to exercise the stomach!

(IRINA exits.

Sound effects off stage: Cheers then the music stops.

All of the guests enter. MARIA runs off again followed by PATAK. The VIOLINIST sets down his instrument and waits for ILONA to serve him wine. BELA sits very closely beside SUSI and lets her drink from his cup. TIBOR joins VIKTOR. VERA hungrily helps herself to bread and pickles. JANOS enters last.)

VIKTOR: That's the life!

JANOS: How about a harvest feast every day?

VIKTOR: If you pay for it, why not?

JANOS: If I were as rich as you are, I'd invite my friends every day to wine and music . . .

TIBOR: And be a poor man very soon.

(IRINA comes with a covered bowl and sets it down on the table before VERA. MARIA and PATAK bring two more bowls and set them down on the other two tables. VERA takes off the lid and sniffs the contents. IRINA sits down beside ISTVAN at the table where PATAK set down a bowl. She stops ISTVAN from getting up.)

IRINA: Not yet. Wait until he's eaten.

(IRINA serves pörkölt from the bowl into the plates of the young people. VERA does the same at her table for VIKTOR and TIBOR—as does MARIA at the third table where she

sits with PATAK and the VIOLINIST.)

VIKTOR: What are you two whispering about? My family always has these secret conversations! Enough, Vera! I know that I have a healthy appetite, but I want to leave some room for the cake.

(All begin to eat except SUSI and BELA too busy flirting to eat. JANOS joins ISTVAN at his table.)

VIKTOR : Say, Istvan, I don't see your little girlfriend. Did she leave you for a wealthier man? Or did you finally realize that there are other skirts to lift? Well? What is it? Aren't you speaking with your old father anymore? That's what happens when you spoil your children. Tell me, haven't I given him everything?

TIBOR: I think youth is always the same. Don't get heated up about it, Viktor. I say: a toast to Viktor!

JANOS: To Irina and Viktor Geza—our gracious hosts!

BELA: To beautiful women.

VIKTOR: I'll drink to that!

JANOS *(softly to ISTVAN)*: I guess, he doesn't know yet.

ISTVAN: Who told you?

JANOS: The Silberhuf family are friends of my parents'.

VIKTOR (*loudly*): Whispering again! Is this the new fashion in Budapest? Out here, in the country, it's still considered rude!

JANOS: Nothing special.

VIKTOR: If it's nothing special, then I'm sure we can all hear it.

IRINA: More pörkölt?

VIKTOR: I want to know what all this whispering is about!

(*Silence.*)

ISTVAN: Arabella Silberhuf and I were married yesterday.

VIKTOR : You idiot! You fired into her belly, or what?!

ISTVAN: If you mean, we're expecting a child -

VIKTOR (*shouting*): Not even you are such an asshole that you'd marry the Jewish slut for any other reason! (*Pause.*) This will be annulled. A few thousand pengö will set the girl up nicely in a shop of her own—that should satisfy the Silber—somethings. Wine, Irina! Give me to drink!

(*He pours and holds up the mug.*)

VIKTOR: Come, Istvan, drink with me! We'll not let this ruin the day. Trust me—I know how to handle this. I too was young once, you know. We're all entitled to make mistakes; right, Tibor? Let's drink to Kuta! To the good life!
ISTVAN: My marriage will not be annulled.
VIKTOR: What do you mean?
ISTVAN: I'm happy to have married Arabella. I'm very happy she agreed to be my wife.

(Behind ISTVAN, ARABELLA -here aged 17- appears at the gate.)

VIKTOR: You're insane!
ISTVAN: I ask you humbly and with all the respect I owe you to accept Arabella as your daughter and to welcome her in this house.
VIKTOR: Do you hear what he wants? Never! Never! Never will this slut enter my house!

(ARABELLA exits)

ISTVAN: Then I have to go.
IRINA: Viktor! I beg you! This is our son!
VIKTOR: If that dirty Jewish whore is more important to him than his family, let him go!

IRINA: How can you? Viktor! Our son. Our only child. Please! You're sending our only son away!

(*She kneels before her husband.*)

IRINA: Please.

> (*VIKTOR gently touches her head and lifts her face.*)

VIKTOR: We no longer have a son.
IRINA: Yes, we do! Look at him! He stands before you. He's your flesh! He's our pride! We made him, Viktor. He's my baby.
VIKTOR (*turning away from her*): You're hysterical, like your son! (*To ISTVAN*) You believe you're the only one she wrapped her legs around? Where are you going? I'm not done yet!
ISTVAN: My wife is waiting.
VIKTOR: Then go.

> (*Exit ISTVAN.*)

IRINA (*softly*): You're cruel.
VIKTOR: You too can leave. Everybody leave the old man! Go!
IRINA: He doesn't need me. He has a wife now and soon a baby. You are depriving me

of my son and my grandchild with your harshness.

Blackout

Film 5

On a white sheet of paper in a manual typewriter, the words

New Romance in 1956

are slowly typed.

EXT. STREETS OF PEST - 1956 - DAY.

Istvan, wearing hat and coat, and Arabella, wearing a coat and with a scarf on her head (the same that hang in the entrance of the apartment), walk along the streets. Istvan takes her by the elbow. Arabella smiles up at him.

INT. AUDITORIUM - DAY

Istvan and Arabella stand before the commemorative plaque reading "1939-1945." Istvan takes a piece of paper and some glue from his coat pocket. He glues the piece of paper over the name "Geza, Istvan." He takes a pencil and writes "élek" [subtitle: "I am alive"] on the paper. Arabella touches the piece of paper and traces the letters of the word.

Act II

Scene 3

<u>Budapest, 1956</u>

Set: The functional gray office 4b from Act I, Scene 3. The absurdly large calendar now has 22 October as the date. SOROS is seated at his desk.

> *ISTVAN and ARABELLA enter, dressed as in Film 5. ARABELLA removes the scarf from her head and folds it with care.*

SOROS: What can I do for you?
ISTVAN (*removes his hat*): Geza. Geza Istvan.
SOROS: So?
ARABELLA: Geza, Arabella. Here are my papers.
ISTVAN: What's all that!
ARABELLA: Birth certificates, marriage, and your . . .
SOROS: Ah, yes. I tried to find this . . . this Kuta. It doesn't exist.
ARABELLA: Destroyed.
SOROS: You knew that!
ARABELLA: My husband didn't.
SOROS: I see. Any relatives?

69

ARABELLA: My husband's parents were killed when a bomb hit the house in Kuta. His uncle lives here in Budapest. Malnak Balasz.

(SOROS takes notes.)

SOROS: Malnak Balasz. Well, Kuta isn't on any map.
ISTVAN: Where did all those people go?
SOROS: I had your papers translated. There are a few points I'd like to go over with you.

(He flips through the folder.)

SOROS According to the papers you handed me, you were sentenced to death, to be executed as an enemy of the Soviet Union. This verdict was changed to twenty-five years . . .
ISTVAN: I got out early. It had to do with world politics rather than good conduct on my part.
SOROS: Yes. You were released a year ago.
ARABELLA: A year ago?
SOROS: You walked into my office last week. Mr. Geza—that year?
ISTVAN: Does it matter? *(Pause.)* I was near Moscow. I worked there.

Blackout

Spot on ISTVAN – Interrogation Scene -

ISTVAN: Near Moscow. *(Pause.)* I worked there. *(Pause.)* Alexandre Stuln. He ran a small school. It closed because there were no students. *(Pause.)* Weiss. I worked with Weiss Arpad. *(Pause.)*The Hungarian paper for prisoners.

ARABELLA: You never wrote. Prisoners were allowed to write. I know that! The Red Cross organized it after 1947! The prisoners wrote! Why didn't you?

ISTVAN: *(to ARABELLA)* I couldn't. *(Pause.)* We were hungry. (*shouts*) Starving! *(He jerks back as if hit.)* Da! Da! *(He listens, cowers, then holds his hands up for water.)* Vada. Water. Please.

ARABELLA *(still in the dark)*: Who stopped you?

> *(ISTVAN is pulled back and forth between the interrogation and his conversation with ARABELLA.)*

ISTVAN: Nobody. I just couldn't. I couldn't. *(Pause.)* I don't know whom she knows. *(Pause.)* I'll never understand the others. How could I write a letter to you, when I could be dead before you get it? *(Pause.)* I did not work for the Germans! *(To*

ARABELLA) I didn't want to write a lie. Don't you understand?
(*Pause*) What was I to write? Was I to write, "I'm fine. See you in twenty-five years. I love you," year after year? Such horrible cards. Censored words of love. Year after year. And if you had met another man, would you have let me know? Would you have the courage to tell a man who is condemned to twenty-five years of forced labor that you're with another man? That you will not be there when I come home? That I have no home? I wanted you to live. (*He listens.*) We paid. My family put up the money and we bought Arabella's life. *(He listens and then whispers.)* I tried to protect the others. We did what we could, it wasn't . . . (*To ARABELLA*) I mean, I wanted you to be free and strong, not sitting in a room waiting for a man who might never come back! I was dead! Do you know how many died every day? (*He listens.*) I don't know who's left. I've just come . . . (*To ARABELLA*) I couldn't care for you. I couldn't help you. (*He listens and slowly nods.)* How will you contact me? (*To ARABELLA*) I couldn't make any

promises. A letter doesn't replace a lover.

ARABELLA: Free? You didn't even know whether I was alive!

(The lights change back to office mood.)

SOROS: How did you survive?

ISTVAN: Translations. I speak fluent Russian. After ten years, I think that's normal.

SOROS: You decided to stay for one more year of your own free will?

ISTVAN: I was afraid. I was afraid to come back. Ten years! That's a very long time!

Blackout

Film 6

White piece of scrap paper covered with illegible notes and doodles. In the upper right corner,

"October, 1956"

is clearly legible. On the bottom of the page the name

"Clara"

and underneath,

"2—Kuta"

are also legible.

EXT. FIELD AND BARN - DAY.

Istvan, wearing hat and coat, walks slowly over the field accompanied by a WOMAN with a tired face - her hands buried deep in the pockets of her coat. He looks around the field like a man looking for something to recognize. Istvan stops and stares sadly at the dilapidated barn. Istvan enters the barn, she hesitates and then follows him.

INT. DILAPIDATED BARN - DAY

Istvan drops down on a pile of moldy
straw. The woman paces nervously
between piles of chopped wood, rusty
metal and an old harness. Her face
is tense. She shivers in the cold.
Istvan reaches out to her. She takes
his hand in hers, caresses it, and
then drops it. She bends down and
gives him a farewell kiss. There are
tears on Istvan's face.

EXT. DILAPIDATED BARN - LATER

The woman walks hurriedly from the
barn.

INT. DILAPIDATED BARN – CONT.

Istvan lies curled up on the pile of
straw.

Act II

Scene 4

<u>Budapest, October 1956</u>

Set: a small café, similar to the one in Film 3. The stage holds table and two chairs; the rest is a painted backdrop.

ARABELLA sits down at the table and clumsily removes her coat and scarf. Feeling chilly, she drapes the coat over her shoulders again. A WAITER approaches.

WAITER: Tesék? [What would you like?]
ARABELLA: Fekete. [Black.]

> *(WAITER nods and exits.*
>
> *ARABELLA takes her time to look around.*
>
> *WAITER returns with a small cup of coffee and a glass of water, serves and exits.*
>
> *ISTVAN enters.)*

ISTVAN: Thank you. Thank you for meeting me here.
ARABELLA: That was a short trip.
ISTVAN: I had to see somebody.

ARABELLA: Why here?

ISTVAN: It's easier to talk here. (*Pause.*) I want to tell you about that year. I didn't, originally. I thought we could just get together again, like it used to be. (*Pause.*) We were happily married, weren't we? (*Pause.*) I was. I was very happy. Now, all I see is pain. I don't even know what I could say or do. (*Pause.*) I'm not responsible for what happened to us.

ARABELLA: I'm trying.

ISTVAN: With your head. I know. But the sorrow's in your heart.

ARABELLA: I'm not a romantic! (*Pause.*) What about the year in Moscow?

ISTVAN: Let me tell you about the ten years in the camps before that. It's important for you to know. I think you need to know so you can understand.

ARABELLA: I don't think this café is open that long.

ISTVAN: I'll be brief. (*Pause.*) I was captured and put on a train. After thirteen days the train stopped. Thirteen days that were an introduction to what was to be my life: twice a day a slice of black bread, a bowl of thin soup, occasionally some hot water. We started with 43 men per wagon and ended with ten less by our arrival. We were allowed to remove the first dead after five days and bury them in shallow graves by the side of the tracks: cholera and typhoid had broken out. (*Pause.*) It would be a long story. (*There is another pause as he drinks from her water.*) That was Krasnokams along the river Kama. We were greeted by Captain Ostapec. Through a translator we were informed that we were to make amends for what the criminal fascist armies had perpetrated on the Soviet people. (*Pause.*) Ten years. One camp, or gupwi, then another: I was just one of about six million prisoners. Lubljanka, Molotov, Krasnogorsk. The labor, the constant hunger, the battle to somehow organize just one more bite of food. (*Pause.*) You've heard all this from others. (*Pause.*) Stories. Now it's a story. My life!

(Silence.)

ARABELLA: I think about it the whole time.
ISTVAN: Yes. I believe you do. (*Pause.*) In the last camp, the last camp I was in before . . . a few months before . . . it was just before I was set free in May 1955 . . . there were also women. There had been women in some of the other camps: Russians. Most of them ignored us. (*Pause.*) This camp also

had female prisoners of war. Not many; most had been sent home earlier.

ARABELLA: What's her name?

ISTVAN: Clara.

ARABELLA: You saw her today.

ISTVAN: A few years older than I am. Hungarian. She had also been there for ten years. (*Pause.*) In a camp, the strong get the females—when there are any. (*Pause.*) After years of starvation, deprived of all human dignity, what is left is an animal with a few basic instincts. (*Pause.*) When we were released, Clara immediately wanted to return to her family. She knew that her husband lived with someone. (*Pause.*) Many knew that the wife or husband who sent them packages had started a new life. I was afraid, Arabella. I was afraid to come back. I wouldn't know where to go, what to do. (*Pause.*) So many years dreaming about that day: freedom!

(*The WAITER enters.*)

WAITER: Tesék?

ISTVAN: Fekete.

(*WAITER exits.*)

ISTVAN: Freedom. I was free and didn't know what to do with it. The freedom to return home! All these fantasies! (*Pause.*) I convinced Clara to stay with me.

ARABELLA: In the Soviet Union.

ISTVAN: I failed. I failed her and I failed you. She wanted to return to her husband and see what she could save. She wanted to love her grown children. (*Pause.*) She doesn't want to see me again.

ARABELLA: And you? What do you want?

ISTVAN: It's not as I had imagined.

(WAITER enters and serves ISTVAN coffee and a glass of water.)

ISTVAN: Köszönöm. [Thank you.]

(WAITER exits.)

ARABELLA: We can't go back, Istvan. None of us can do that.

ISTVAN: Clara has nothing to do with my feelings for you.

ARABELLA: I think I know that.

(ISTVAN tries to raise his cup. His hands shake violently and the hot coffee spills on his coat.

ARABELLA takes a handkerchief from her coat pocket, dips it into her water glass and wipes the stain.)

ISTVAN: I don't know you anymore.

ARABELLA: I was a child when we were married. I'm a middle-aged woman now and you weren't here for my passing from one to the other.

Blackout

Act 3

Scene 1

<u>Budapest, Hungary, Winter of 1989</u>

The small apartment of ARABELLA GEZA.

Set suggestions: all surfaces are now covered with photographs: MICHAEL as a baby, as a small child, as a youth, and as a young man.

> *ARABELLA, wearing a black dress, kneels on the floor taking more framed photographs from a carton. She carefully wipes the dust off each one as she takes it out and then looks for a place to put it. The door opens and ISTVAN, elegantly dressed in a suit and tie, his coat and scarf, enters.*

ISTVAN: It was open. *(Pause.)* You should lock the door. Anyone could just walk in.

> *(He closes the door.)*

ARABELLA: The dust.

ISTVAN: I thought, we were going out to dinner. I really want to take you somewhere nice, Bella. Can we go? I made a reservation.
ARABELLA: I already ate.

(Silence.)

ISTVAN: You're looking very elegant, Arabella. (*Pause.*) I reserved a table for us at the Hilton. Have you been there?
ARABELLA: No.
ISTVAN: I don't understand. We agreed this morning. I asked you this morning to come and have dinner with me tonight and . . .
ARABELLA: I know. (*Pause.*) I took a bath and put on this dress. My hands are all dirty now. (*Pause.*) Do you go?
ISTVAN: No. (*Pause.*) Did you really eat?
ARABELLA: You're also looking very elegant. (*Pause.*) I thought you also went. There are flowers . . .
ISTVAN: I have them delivered.
ARABELLA: November. Every November there are fresh flowers.
ISTVAN: I haven't forgotten. I couldn't.
ARABELLA: I go every week. I take the bus. It's a bus full of old women, each with a small bunch of flowers in her hand. Old hands. Some go to talk to their husbands,

but most visit the graves of their children. (*Pause.*) He was all we had, Istvan.

> (*ARABELLA cries and ISTVAN gently puts his arms around her.*)

ISTVAN: Let the past rest, little Bella. We're living now.

ARABELLA: It's not the past. It was this morning and yesterday morning and it will be every morning until I take my place beside him.

ISTVAN: Michael died more than thirty years ago!

> (*ARABELLA pushes him away and returns to wiping photographs.*)

ISTVAN: It was an accident!

ARABELLA: There were no accidents in those days! A Soviet tank is not an accident! (*Pause.*) Days we couldn't mention for thirty-three years.

ISTVAN: Our son was not a hero. He was there accidentally. I don't think he knew . . .

ARABELLA: What do we know? We saw him dead. We saw this beautiful child as a corpse.

ISTVAN: For god's sake let go!

Blackout

Film 7

White sheet of paper in a manual typewriter. The name

Michael

<u>Collage</u> of newspaper headlines pertaining to the beginning of the Hungarian uprising of October 23, 24, and 25, 1956.

EXT. PARK BENCH BY PETOFI STATUE - DAY.

Istvan sits on the bench with an open photo album on his knees.

<u>Insert</u>

Black & white photographs of a village in Hungary in the 1930s.

Black & white. photograph of Michael as a small boy on Istvan's lap.

Back to scene

MICHAEL sits beside ISTVAN on the bench. ISTVAN puts the open album on MICHAEL's lap. MICHAEL looks lost. ISTVAN takes the album back.

Act III

Scene 2

<u>Budapest, Hungary, in October of 1956</u>

The apartment of ARABELLA GEZA.
Lights come up as the entrance door is closed.
> *ISTVAN and ARABELLA sharing a newspaper. ARABELLA is dressed in a business suit, ISTVAN wears only shirt and trousers—his feet are bare. PROHASZKA tidies MICHAEL's half empty glass of milk and plate onto a tray.*

ISTVAN: How old is Michael?
ARABELLA: You've forgotten?!
ISTVAN: I mean, mentally.
PROHASZKA: More coffee?

(She exits with the empty pot.)

ISTVAN: So?
ARABELLA: Some say six. Others think twelve. The average evaluation is about ten.
ISTVAN: How many doctors did you consult? Specialists at the university?
ARABELLA: Too many. Have you finished? I've got an appointment at eight-thirty.

ISTVAN: I don't even know what you do. I'm sorry—I've only been talking about myself.

ARABELLA: Divorces and minors. Our society thinks women can't handle anything more serious. I don't mean family law isn't serious. Children are serious. They often need protection. But I hate handling divorces. All that emotional dirty laundry. It used to embarrass me—now it bores me. (*Pause.*) But those are the prejudices: emotional women, unemotional men.

ISTVAN: When did you get your degree?

ARABELLA: It wasn't easy. The wife of a son from a bourgeois family wasn't exactly on the top of the list of people they wished to educate . . . but your uncle Balasz helped. (*Pause.*) He's over seventy now and doesn't like being old. He hates it! There are no mirrors in his home. A barber comes to shave him once a week.

(ISTVAN *helps her into her coat*)

ISTVAN: He lives alone?

ARABELLA: He made it possible for his lover to emigrate to Australia. He's been alone since.

(*PROHASZKA enters.*)

PROHASZKA: What about the coffee?

ARABELLA: I'll drink it cold later: it keeps my complexion fresh. Could you go over to Mr. Malnak and invite him to join us for lunch? And bring him my newspaper. He'll protest, but I know he'll read it. We'll have the ham.

ISTVAN: Ham?

ARABELLA: A grateful client.

ISTVAN: When did you start eating pork?

(PROHASZKA exits.)

ARABELLA : I was hungry.

ISTVAN: Have you lost your faith?

ARABELLA: What do you believe in?

ISTVAN: I'll go and invite Uncle Balasz.

Blackout

Film 8

A white sheet of paper in a manual typewriter:

 Michael

is slowly typed, and then the paper is ripped out.

COLLAGE

handwritten evaluations of MICHAEL's condition on stationary bearing hospital names and the names of psychiatric doctors. The dates in the upper left corner of the letters go from 1946 to 1954. The words "trauma", "traumatizmus" appear several times in every letter. At the bottom of every letter is the following statement: "At this time, there is nothing more to do for the patient. We recommend institution- alizing." (in Hungarian with subtitles.)

INT. MICHAEL's BEDROOM - 1956 - Day

A young boy's bedroom. A model train set from the 1950's crisscrosses.

Michael sits in the middle of the room and moves the trains around on the tracks. He looks up and smiles.

MCHAEL's POV

Istvan stands in the door.

BACK TO SCENE

MICHAEL waves ISTVAN over and holds up an engine. ISTVAN kneels down beside MICHAEL.

Act III

Scene 3

Budapest, Hungary, in November of 1956.

Set: The apartment of ARABELLA GEZA.

ARABELLA stands at the window.
ISTVAN enters with a pot of coffee.

ARABELLA: Madness! Hungarians shooting their own people. It's mad out there. I doubt Prohaszka will come. Where's Michael?
ISTVAN: In his room.
ARABELLA: Nobody knows what's going on. I tried to listen to the BBC. The reports are confusing. Maybe this will end soon. Maybe the Russians will give us some freedom.
ISTVAN: Not the ones I've met.
ARABELLA: The rest of the world won't leave them any choice.
ISTVAN: Don't forget the Communists in power—Hungarians who are interested in holding on to their positions.

(Silence.)

ISTVAN: When did you last have Michael examined?

ARABELLA: Two years ago.

ISTVAN: Two years! Things have advanced -

ARABELLA: When they gave me my son back, he spent weeks in his room whimpering, wetting himself, hiding his face from the light, pulling away from me—from all people. I don't know what they did to Michael—perhaps it's better that I don't.

ISTVAN: So this is it? You're just going to leave him as he is?

ARABELLA: I'm not even going to discuss this! It's not Michael you care about—it's you! You're ashamed to have a handicapped son.

ISTVAN: You don't want to understand me, do you? If you did, you'd have to care again. Trust again. I would be real. (*Pause.*) You understood me before. When I had worries, you hugged me. Love energy was what we called it.

ARABELLA: That's not fair.

ISTVAN: You laughed a lot in those days.

ARABELLA: It's hard to laugh when bathing a growing man, changing his sheets every night, teaching and re-teaching him how to dress himself . . .

ISTVAN: I'll help! You'll laugh again, Bella.

ARABELLA: Bella was abandoned eleven years ago.

ISTVAN: I didn't leave you! The war separated us—us and millions of other men and women. (*Pause.*) Is there another man in your life?
ARABELLA: He's twenty years old.

(Sound effects: shots in the distance.)

ISTVAN: Give me a chance! I need time. I have so much to catch up on! I have to get my bearings in this new world. Please. (*Pause.*) I've lived through years of . . . seen torture . . .pain . . . your worst nightmare can't create it! These experiences have left their mark. Ten years of my life, Arabella. Ten years. I have to learn to be normal again. I don't want to hurt you. I don't want to hurt Michael.
ARABELLA: I'll keep that in mind.

(ARABELLA gets her coat. ISTVAN follows her.)

ARABELLA: What more do you want, Istvan? The family has embraced the returning father.

ISTVAN: You're making me responsible for the war! I didn't want a war! I didn't want to be a soldier! I didn't want to waste the best years of my life as a prisoner! I wanted to live my life with you, here in Budapest. I wanted to spend my life caring for you and Michael.

ARABELLA: And Clara? (*Pause.*) I have to see whether my office still stands. You want to take care of Michael? Look after him until I get back.

> (*ARABELLA exits. ISTVAN goes back to the table, pours himself coffee and flips through the album. MICHAEL comes from his room, dressed in a dark blue railroad worker's uniform.*)

ISTVAN: Good morning, Michael. Coffee?

MICHAEL: Where's Prohaszka? She makes hot milk . . .

ISTVAN: Prohaszka isn't coming today. Join me for breakfast. There's no work today.

> (*Sound effects: shots in the distance, people chanting.*)

MICHAEL: What's this noise? Why can't I go to work?

ISTVAN: There's an uprising. Hungarians are trying to get rid of the Russians. And there's a strike. Nobody is working.

(Istvan closes the window. Sound effects: shots in the distance.)

MICHAEL: Mom went to work. I heard the door.
ISTVAN: She went to her office. She'll be right back. Milk?
Michael: Why do we want to get rid of the Russians?

(ISTVAN contemplates the question as Michael laps his milk like a kitten from the cup.)

ISTVAN: Because they forgot to feed the Hungarians. Nobody likes to go hungry.

(Sound effects: shots. Michael runs to the window.)

MICHAEL: Will mom be back? Are they shooting? Are the Russians shooting at us? They're shooting my mom! The Russians are bad! They're shooting!

(ISTVAN drags MICHAEL from the window)

ISTVAN: I don't know who's shooting. We can't see from here, Michael. Get away from this window. All shooting is dangerous. Don't you remember hearing gunfire before? There was the war, Michael, when you were a boy.

MICHAEL: No.

ISTVAN: You were a little boy. Remember, I wore a uniform. You liked my uniform. You even tried it on. It was so big! The jacket touched your feet. And you were sad because you couldn't play outside—it was too dangerous. We had to keep you indoors and when there were air raids, we all had to go down to the cellar . . .

(*He flips open an album and points at a photograph.*)

ISTVAN: This is your grandmother. She came to take you to Kuta so you could play outside again. Have you really forgotten?

MICHAEL: Uncle Balasz and Mom sometimes talk about the war, but I don't remember.

ISTVAN: You were in Kuta, Michael. Our family home. You were there! See, the tall trees on the sides of the road and the big white house . . . behind are stables for horses. And all around, there are fields. . I

climbed these trees when I was a little boy. And this is a picture of my favorite horse. . .
MICHAEL: What was his name? Were you a good rider? Did you go over really high jumps?

(Sound effects: a shell explodes very close. The window rattles from the vibrations.)

MICHAEL (*jumps up and screams*): Run!
ISTVAN: Better get down to the cellar.

(ISTVAN exits.

Sound effects: gun fire.)

MICHAEL: Bombs! Bombs! The plane is dropping bombs! We have to run to the house! We'll be safe in the house.

(ISTVAN stands frozen in the door to the master bedroom watching MICHAEL.

Sound effect: another shell explodes.

The window shatters and dust billows in.)

MICHAEL (*crying hysterically*): Granny! I can't run so fast! Grandpa! We have to find Grandpa! We have to get to the house!

(MICHAEL exits.

ISTVAN stands frozen a few moments as dust continues to billow in through the shattered window.

Sound effects: gun fire and another shell exploding.

ISTVAN grabs his coat.)

Blackout

Film 9

COLLAGE

Newspaper headlines from October 27-November 1, 1956 re. Hungarian uprising.

EXT. STREETS OF BUDAPEST – DAY.

PEOPLE stand huddled in small groups by street corners and house entrances.

STREET BARRICADE.

A group of STUDENTS crouch behind a barricade of furniture and scrap parts. Their faces are determined. A YOUNG WOMAN shows others her machine gun.

ISTVAN passes. A woman runs after him and taps him on the shoulder. Istvan freezes in his tracks, then turns very slowly to her. His face shows fear. The woman shakes her head apologetically.

A CROWD OF ANGRY PEOPLE runs down the street.

Istvan stands alone at the end of the street.

ISTVAN's POV

Michael comes running around a corner and is swept along by the crowd.

Back to scene.

Istvan runs after Michael.

The crowd runs.

Act III

Scene 4

Budapest, November 1956; Winter 1989

Projections on multiple screens show images of the uprising: barricades, a decapitated statue of Stalin, tanks, dead civilians lying on the streets.

> *Men and women run back and forth across the stage, fleeing from the noise of gun fire, shells, and approaching tanks that comes first from stage left, then from stage right.*

> *MICHAEL runs on and grabs the hand of an OLDER WOMAN.*

MICHAEL: We have to get to Kuta.
OLDER WOMAN (*extremely frightened*): Let me go!
MICHAEL: We have to find Grandpa!
OLDER WOMAN: Let me go, boy! I've got to get to my children!

> *(OLDER WOMAN yanks herself free and runs off.*

> *MICHAEL, completely bewildered, stops a YOUNG MAN.)*

MICHAEL: Which way is Kuta?

YOUNG MAN: Sing along! Russians out! Russians out! Russians out!

(Three MEN join the YOUNG MAN and advance together, chanting.)

CHOIR OF MEN: Russians out! Russians out! Russians out!

(They exit chanting.)

MICHAEL *(singing alone)*: Russians out! Russians out!

(MICHAEL starts to run.

Three armed YOUNG WOMEN enter.

MICHAEL barges into one YOUNG WOMAN.)

MICHAEL: Where's Kuta? It's safe in Kuta.
FIRST YOUNG WOMAN: Petöfi Sandor statue. All students are at the Petöfi Sandor statue!
SECOND YOUNG WOMAN: Hurry! Don't stand there! God! Look!

(Sound effects of approaching tanks grows louder.

Three YOUNG WOMEN run off in a panic.

Men and women run in panic.

MICHAEL stops a MAN.)

MICHAEL: Where is the Petöfi . . . ?

(The man punches MICHAEL.

Screens change to city streets with tanks approaching.

Another man runs past Michael.)

RUNNING MAN: Run! Run, boy!

(MICHAEL clings to the MAN's arm.)

MICHAEL: I have to get to Kuta!

(The MAN half drags MICHAEL with him.

Sound effect of tanks extremely close.)

MAN: Where they've been, there's nothing left!

(MICHAEL drops the MAN's arm.)

MICHAEL: It's my home! I'm safe there!

(The MAN runs off.

A WOMAN with a gun stops and turns towards the screens of tanks blocking the city streets.

WOMAN: Bastards! Traitors! Traitors!

WOMAN tries to fire the gun. It's not loaded. She drops the gun and runs off. MICHAEL picks up the gun and walks toward the approaching tanks, oblivious of the panic around him.

Sound effects: terrifying sounds of war. Heavy tanks running over barricades.

Blackout

Silence.

Slowly the lights come up. They reveal empty screens.

A MAN kneels next to MICHAEL, who lies in agony. The WOMAN who dropped the gun slowly approaches.

WOMAN: Is he dead? Oh, my God!
MAN: His heart's still beating.
WOMAN: I'll get help.

(The woman exits)

MICHAEL: You're so heavy, Grandpa. Granny, say something! So heavy.
MAN: Somebody'll be here in a moment. Somebody'll come and help.
MICHAEL: It hurts so.

(The lights dim to near darkness.

White screens are set up around Michael.

ARABELLA runs to the screens as ISTVAN and a DOCTOR step out from behind the screens and stop her.)

ARABELLA: Where is Michael?
DOCTOR: Mrs. Geza, I am very sorry . . .
ARABELLA: Where is Michael?! I want to-
DOCTOR: There is nothing-
ARABELLA: I want to see my son!
DOCTOR: His heart's still beating, but . . .

(ISTVAN forcefully holds ARABELLA back.)

ARABELLA: Michael needs me!
ISTVAN: Arabella, please. . .
ARABELLA: Let me go!

(ISTVAN and ARABELLA struggle. She pushes him violently away and goes behind the screen.)

DOCTOR: No mother should see her child like that.

(DOCTOR exits.

ISTVAN stands alone in front of the screens. He changes to ISTVAN aged 74.

Slow fade and only a small light is visible through the screen.

The small light goes suddenly off.

ARABELLA appears wearing the black dress from Act III. Scene 1.

Soft spot on ISTVAN and ARABELLA. ISTVAN puts his arms around ARABELLA to console her. He holds her silently for a moment.)

ISTVAN: Did he say anything?

(ARABELLA shakes her head.)

ARABELLA: Why did he run out? What was he doing on the streets?

ISTVAN: Michael wanted to find you. I tried to stop him, but he pushed past me. I tried to find him on the streets . . .

ARABELLA (*a tired 71 years old*): For thirty-three years now I wake up knowing my son died looking for me. If I had stayed home . . . if only I had stayed . . . but he was on the streets and he had a gun . . . a stupid, empty gun and he tried to stop a tank with an empty gun! This is the guilt I live with. Every day, I know my son died looking for me.

ISTVAN: It's not your fault, Bella! Michael wasn't on the streets looking for you! He was trying to get to Kuta! You had left for your office and the street battles started. Michael and I were talking. I tried to explain who I was, where I came from . . . I thought that if he remembered Kuta . . . I thought it would cure him. I didn't have the courage to tell you, then. I tried to stop him, Bella. I tried to stop Michael from running out the door, but he heard explosions and something changed in him.

ISTVAN: If only I hadn't talked about Kuta. I thought Kuta was the safest place for our son when the war broke out—and what happened? And—again—I thought if only he would remember Kuta he would become normal. If anyone is responsible, I suppose I am. That's why I left then. I couldn't look at your pain and know I had caused it.

ARABELLA: You left me to mourn alone.

ISTVAN: I can't mourn the way you do, Bella. I wanted to live. I want to live now. I was so happy when you called. When I said, there is hope now, I was talking about us. Holding you last night was the best night of the last thirty-three years. I want more nights like that. I want to wake up and see you beside me, just as we planned before war and fear destroyed all our dreams. I want joy. I want just a little corner of joy with you.

> *(Arabella remains silent. Istvan, defeated exits leaving the door open. Arabella goes to close the door, then throws it fully open.)*

ARABELLA (*calls*): Hey, Istvan. Aren't you taking me to dinner? What?

BLACKOUT

About the Author

Johanna Miklós was born in Munich, Germany but now calls the USA home. She has a MFA in playwrighting from The Catholic University of America and has worked in Theatre and other industries in Germany, France and the USA.